The White Cliffs

by
Alice Duer Miller

Printed on acid free ANSI archival quality paper.
ISBN: 978-1-78139-194-5

Contents

I

I have loved England, dearly and deeply,
Since that first morning, shining and pure,
The white cliffs of Dover I saw, rising steeply
Out of the sea that once made her secure.

I had no thought then of husband or lover,
I was a traveler, the guest of a week;
Yet when they pointed "the white cliffs of Dover,"
Startled I found there were tears on my cheek.

I have loved England, and still as a stranger,
Here is my home, and I still am alone.
Now in her hour of trial and danger,
Only the English are really her own.

II

It happened the first evening I was there.
Someone was giving a ball in Belgrave Square.
At Belgrave Square, that most Victorian spot.--
Lives there a novel-reader who has not
At some time wept for those delightful girls,
Daughters of dukes, prime ministers, and earls,
In bonnets, berthas, bustles, buttoned basques,
Hiding behind their pure Victorian masks
Hearts just as hot--hotter perhaps than those
Whose owners now abandon hats and hose.
Who has not wept for Lady Joan or Jill
Loving against her noble parent's will
A handsome guardsman, and to her alarm
Feels her hand kissed behind a potted palm
At Lady Ivry's ball the dreadful night
Before his regiment goes off to fight;
And sees him the next morning, in the park,
Complete in busbee, marching to embark.
I had read freely, even as a child,
Not only Meredith and Oscar Wilde
But many novels of an earlier day--
Ravenshoe, *Can You Forgive Her*, *Vivien Grey*,
Ouida, The Duchess, Broughton's *Red As A Rose*,
Guy Livingstone, Whyte-Melville--Heaven knows
What others. Now, I thought, I was to see
Their habitat, though like the Miller of Dee,
I cared for none, and no one cared for me.

III

A light blue carpet on the stair
And tall young footmen everywhere,
Tall young men with English faces
Standing rigidly in their places,
Rows and rows of them stiff and staid
In powder and breeches and bright gold braid;
And high above them on the wall
Hung other English faces--all
Part of the pattern of English life--
General Sir Charles, and his pretty wife,
Admirals, Lord Lieutenants of Shires,
Men who were served by these footmen's sires
At their great parties--none of them knowing
How soon or late they would all be going
In plainer dress to a sterner strife--
Another pattern of English life.

I went up the stairs between them all,
Strange and frightened and shy and small,
And as I entered the ballroom door,
Saw something I never had seen before
Except in portraits--a stout old guest
With a broad blue ribbon across his breast--
That blue as deep as the Southern sea,
Bluer than skies can ever be--
The Countess of Salisbury--Edward the Third--
No damn merit--the Duke--I heard
My own voice saying: "Upon my word,
The garter!" and clapped my hands like a child.

Someone beside me turned and smiled,
And looking down at me said: "I fancy
You're Bertie's Australian cousin Nancy.
He told me to tell you that he'd be late
At the Foreign Office, and not to wait
Supper for him, but to go with me,
And try to behave as if I were he."

I should have told him on the spot
That I had no cousin--that I was not
Australian Nancy--that my name
Was Susan Dunne, and that I came
From a small white town on a deep-cut bay
In the smallest state in the U.S.A.
I meant to tell him, but changed my mind--
I needed a friend, and he seemed kind;
So I put my gloved hand into his glove,
And we danced together--and fell in love.

IV

Young and in love--how magical the phrase!
How magical the fact! Who has not yearned
Over young lovers when to their amaze
They fall in love, and find their love returned,
And the lights brighten, and their eyes are clear
To see God's image in their common clay.
Is it the music of the spheres they hear?
Is it the prelude to that noble play,
The drama of Joined Lives? Ah, they forget
They cannot write their parts; the bell has rung,
The curtain rises, and the stage is set
For tragedy--they were in love and young.

V

We went to the tower,
  We went to the zoo,
We saw every flower
  In the gardens at Kew.
We saw King Charles a-prancing
  On his long tailed horse,
And thought him more entrancing
  Than better kings, of course.
At a strange early hour,
  In St. James's palace yard,
We watched in a shower
  The changing of the guard.
And I said, what a pity,
  To have just a week to spend,
When London is a city
  Whose beauties never end!

VI

When the sun shines on England, it atones
  For low-hung leaden skies, and rain and dim
Moist fogs that paint the verdure on her stones
  And fill her gentle rivers to the brim.

When the sun shines on England, shafts of light
  Fall on far towers and hills and dark old trees,
And hedge-bound meadows of a green as bright--
  As bright as is the blue of tropic seas.

When the sun shines, it is as if the face
  Of some proud man relaxed his haughty stare,
And smiled upon us with a sudden grace,
  Flattering because its coming is so rare.

9

VII

The English are frosty
  When you're no kith or kin
Of theirs, but how they alter
  When once they take you in!
The kindest, the truest,
  The best friends ever known,
It's hard to remember
  How they froze you to a bone.
They showed me all London,
  Johnnie and his friends;
They took me to the country
  For long week ends;
I never was so happy,
  I never had such fun,
I stayed many weeks in England
  Instead of just one.

VIII

John had one of those English faces
  That always were and will always be
Found in the cream of English places
  Till England herself sink into the sea--
A blond, bowed face with prominent eyes
  A little bit bluer than English skies.

You see it in ruffs and suits of armor,
  You see it in wigs of many styles,
Soldier and sailor, judge and farmer--
  That face has governed the British Isles,
By the power, for good or ill bestowed,
  Only on those who live by code.

Oh, that inflexible code of living,
  That seems so easy and unconstrained,
The Englishman's code of taking and giving
  Rights and privileges pre-ordained,
Based since English life began
  On the prime importance of being a man.

IX

And what a voice he had--gentle, profound,
Clear masculine!--I melted at the sound.

Oh, English voices, are there any words
Those tones to tell, those cadences to teach!
As song of thrushes is to other birds,
So English voices are to other speech;
Those pure round "o's"--those lovely liquid "l's"
Ring in the ears like sound of Sabbath bells.

Yet I have loathed those voices when the sense
Of what they said seemed to me insolence,
As if the dominance of the whole nation
Lay in that clear correct enunciation.

Many years later, I remember when
One evening I overheard two men
In Claridge's--white waistcoats, coats I know
Were built in Bond Street or in Savile Row--
So calm, so confident, so finely bred--
Young gods in tails--and this is what they said:
"Not your first visit to the States?"
                    "Oh no,
I'd been in Canada two years ago."
Good God, I thought, have they not heard that we
Were those queer colonists who would be free,
Who took our desperate chance, and fought and won
Under a colonist called Washington?

One does not lose one's birthright, it appears.
I had been English then for many years.

X

We went down to Cambridge,
  Cambridge in the spring.
In a brick court at twilight
  We heard the thrushes sing,
And we went to evening service
  In the chapel of the King.

The library of Trinity,
  The quadrangle of Clare,
John bought a pipe from Bacon,
  And I acquired there
The Anecdotes of Painting
From a handcart in the square.

The playing fields at sunset
  Were vivid emerald green,
The elms were tall and mighty,
  And many youths were seen,
Carefree young gentlemen
  In the Spring of Fourteen.

XI

London, just before dawn--immense and dark--
  Smell of wet earth and growth from the empty park,
Pall Mall vacant--Whitehall deserted. Johnnie and I
  Strolling together, averse to saying good-by--
Strolling away from some party in silence profound,
  Only far off in Mayfair, piercing, the sound
Of a footman's whistle--the rhythm of hoofs on wood,
  Further and further away. . . .
                And now we stood
On a bridge, where a poet came to keep
  Vigil while all the city lay asleep--
Westminster Bridge--and soon the sun would rise,
  And I should see it with my very eyes!
Yes, now it came--a broad and awful glow
  Out of the violet mists of dawn. "Ah, no,"
I said, "earth hath not anything to show
  More fair--changed though it be--than this."
A curious background surely for a kiss--
  Our first--Westminster Bridge at break of day--
Settings by Wordsworth, as John used to say.

XII

Why do we fall in love? I do believe
  That virtue is the magnet, the small vein
Of ore, the spark, the torch that we receive
  At birth, and that we render back again.
That drop of godhood, like a precious stone,
  May shine the brightest in the tiniest flake.
Lavished on saints, to sinners not unknown;
  In harlot, nun, philanthropist, and rake,
It shines for those who love; none else discern
  Evil from good; Man's fall did not bestow
That threatened wisdom; blindly still we yearn
  After a virtue that we do not know,
Until our thirst and longing rise above
  The barriers of reason--and we love.

XIII

And still I did not see my life was changed,
Utterly different--by this love estranged
Forever and ever from my native land;
That I was now of that unhappy band
Who lose the old, and cannot gain the new
However loving and however true
To their new duties. I could never be
An English woman, there was that in me
Puritan, stubborn, that would not agree
To English standards, though I did not see
The truth, because I thought them, good or ill,
So great a people--and I think so still.

But a day came when I was forced to face
Facts. I was taken down to see the place,
The family place in Devon--and John's mother.
"Of course, you understand," he said, "my brother
Will have the place." He smiled; he was so sure
The world was better for primogeniture.
And yet he loved that place, as Englishmen
Do love their native countryside, and when
The day should be as it was sure to be--
When this was home no more to him--when he
Could go there only when his brother's wife
Should ask him--to a room not his--his life
Would shrink and lose its meaning. How unjust,
I thought. Why do they feel it must
Go to that idle, insolent eldest son?
Well, in the end it went to neither one.

XIV

A red brick manor house in Devon,
  In a beechwood of old gray trees,
Ivy climbing to the clustered chimneys,
  Rustling in the wet south breeze.
Gardens trampled down by Cromwell's army,
  Orchards of apple trees and pears,
Casements that had looked for the Armada,
  And a ghost on the stairs.

XV

Johnnie's mother, the Lady Jean,
  Child of a penniless Scottish peer,
Was handsome, worn high-colored, lean,
  With eyes like Johnnie's--more blue and clear--
Like bubbles of glass in her fine tanned face.
  Quiet, she was, and so at ease,
So perfectly sure of her rightful place
  In the world that she felt no need to please.
I did not like her--she made me feel
  Talkative, restless, unsure, as if
I were a cross between parrot and eel.
  I thought her blank and cold and stiff.

XVI

And presently she said as they
Sooner or later always say:
"You're an American, Miss Dunne?
Really you do not speak like one."
She seemed to think she'd said a thing
Both courteous and flattering.
I answered, though my wrists were weak
With anger: "Not at all, I speak--
At least I've always thought this true--
As educated people do
In any country--even mine."
"Really?" I saw her head incline,
I saw her ready to assert
Americans are easily hurt.

XVII

Strange to look back to the days
So long ago
When a friend was almost a foe,
When you hurried to find a phrase
For your easy light dispraise
Of a spirit you did not know,
A nature you could not plumb
In the moment of meeting,
Not guessing a day would come
When your heart would ache to hear
Other men's tongues repeating
Those same light phrases that jest and jeer
At a friend now grown so dear--so dear.
Strange to remember long ago
When a friend was almost a foe.

XVIII

I saw the house with its oaken stair,
  And the Tudor Rose on the newel post,
The paneled upper gallery where
  They told me you heard the family ghost--
"A gentle unhappy ghost who sighs
Outside one's door on the night one dies."

"Not," Lady Jean explained, "at all
  Like the ghost at my father's place, St. Kitts,
That clanks and screams in the great West Hall,
  And frightens strangers out of their wits."
I smiled politely, not thinking I
Would hear one midnight that long sad sigh.

I saw the gardens, after our tea
  (Crumpets and marmalade, toast and cake)
And Drake's Walk, leading down to the sea;
  Lady Jean was startled I'd heard of Drake,
For the English always find it a mystery
That Americans study English history.

I saw the picture of every son--
  Percy, the eldest, and John; and Bill
In Chinese Customs, and the youngest one
  Peter, the sailor, at Osborne still;
And the daughter, Enid, married, alas,
To a civil servant in far Madras.

A little thing happened, just before
  We left--the evening papers came;
John, flicking them over to find a score,
  Spoke for the first time a certain name--
The name of a town in a distant land
Etched on our hearts by a murderer's hand.

Mother and son exchanged a glance,
  A curious glance of strength and dread.

I thought: what matter to them if Franz
  Ferdinand dies? One of them said:
"This might be serious."
                    "Yes, you're right."
The other answered, "It really might."

XIX

Dear John:
            I'm going home. I write to say
Good-by. My boat train leaves at break of day;
It will be gone when this is in your hands.
I've had enough of lovely foreign lands,
Sightseeing, strangers, holiday and play;
I'm going home to those who think the way
I think, and speak as I do. Will you try
To understand that this must be good-by?
We are both rooted deeply in the soil
Of our own countries. But I could not spoil
Our happy memories with the stress and strain
Of parting; if we never meet again,
Be sure I shall remember till I die
Your love, your laugh, your kindness. But--good-by.
Please do not hate me; give the devil his due,
This is an act of courage.
                    Always,
                        Sue.

XX

The boat train rattling
  Through the green countryside;
A girl within it battling
  With her tears and pride.
The Southampton landing,
  Porters, neat and quick,
And a young man standing,
  Leaning on his stick.
"Oh, John, John, you shouldn't
  Have come this long way. . . ."
"Did you really think I wouldn't
  Be here to make you stay?"
I can't remember whether
  There was much stress and strain,
But presently together,
  We were traveling back again.

XXI

The English love their country with a love
Steady, and simple, wordless, dignified;
I think it sets their patriotism above
All others. We Americans have pride--
We glory in our country's short romance.
We boast of it and love it. Frenchmen, when
The ultimate menace comes, will die for France
Logically as they lived. But Englishmen
Will serve day after day, obey the law,
And do dull tasks that keep a nation strong.
Once I remember in London how I saw
Pale shabby people standing in a long
Line in the twilight and the misty rain
To pay their tax. I then saw England plain.

XXII

Johnnie and I were married. England then
Had been a week at war, and all the men
Wore uniform, as English people can,
Unconscious of it. Percy, the best man,
As thin as paper and as smart as paint,
Bade us good-by with admirable restraint,
Went from the church to catch his train to hell;
And died--saving his batman from a shell.

XXIII

We went down to Devon,
  In a warm summer rain,
Knowing that our happiness
  Might never come again;
I, not forgetting,
  "Till death us do part,"
Was outrageously happy
  With death in my heart.

Lovers in peacetime
  With fifty years to live,
Have time to tease and quarrel
  And question what to give;
But lovers in wartime
  Better understand
The fullness of living,
  With death close at hand.

XXIV

My father wrote me a letter--
My father, scholarly, indolent, strong,
Teaching Greek better
Than high-school students repay--
Teaching Greek in the winter, but all summer long
Sailing a yawl in Narragansett Bay;
Happier perhaps when I was away,
Free of an anxious daughter,
He could sail blue water
Day after day,
Beyond Brenton Reef Lightship, and Beavertail,
Past Cuttyhunk to catch a gale
Off the Cape, while he thought of Hellas and Troy,
Chanting with joy
Greek choruses--those lines that he said
Must be written some day on a stone at his head:
"But who can know
As the long years go
That to live is happy, has found his heaven."
My father, so far away--
I thought of him, in Devon,
Anchoring in a blind fog in Boothbay.

XXV

"So, Susan, my dear," the letter began,
"You've fallen in love with an Englishman.
Well, they're a manly, attractive lot,
If you happen to like them, which I do not.
I am a Yankee through and through,
And I don't like them, or the things they do.
Whenever it's come to a knock-down fight
With us, they were wrong, and we were right;
If you don't believe me, cast your mind
Back over history, what do you find?
They certainly had no justification
For that maddening plan to impose taxation
Without any form of representation.
Your man may be all that a man should be,
Only don't you bring him back to me
Saying he can't get decent tea--
He could have got his tea all right
In Boston Harbor a certain night,
When your great-great-grandmother--also a Sue--
Shook enough tea from her husband's shoe
To supply her house for a week or two.
The war of 1812 seems to me
About as just as a war could be.
How could we help but come to grips
With a nation that stopped and searched our ships,
And took off our seamen for no other reason
Except that they needed crews that season.
I can get angry still at the tale
Of their letting the *Alabama* sail,
And Palmerston being insolent
To Lincoln and Seward over the *Trent*.
All very long ago, you'll say,
But whenever I go up Boston-way,
I drive through Concord--that neck of the wood,
Where once the embattled farmers stood,
And I think of Revere, and the Old North Steeple,
And I say, by heck, we're the only people

Who licked them not only once, but twice.
Never forget it--that's my advice.
They have their points--they're honest and brave,
Loyal and sure--as sure as the grave;
They make other nations seem pale and flighty,
But they do think England is God almighty,
And you must remind them now and then
That other countries breed other men.
From all of which you will think me rather
Unjust. I am.
             Your devoted
                Father.

XXVI

I read, and saw my home with sudden yearning--
  The small white wooden house, the grass-green door,
My father's study with the fire burning,
  And books piled on the floor.

I saw the moon-faced clock that told the hours,
  The crimson Turkey carpet, worn and frayed,
The heavy dishes--gold with birds and flowers--
  Fruits of the China trade.

I saw the jack-o'-lanterns, friendly, frightening,
  Shine from our gateposts every Halloween;
I saw the oak tree, shattered once by lightning,
  Twisted, stripped clean.

I saw the Dioscuri--two black kittens,
  Stalking relentlessly an empty spool;
I saw a little girl in scarlet mittens
  Trudging through snow to school.

XXVII

John read the letter with his lovely smile.
"Your father has a vigorous English style,
And what he says is true, upon my word;
But what's this war of which I never heard?
We didn't fight in 1812."

                "Yes, John,
That was the time when you burnt Washington."
"We couldn't have, my dear. . . ."
                    "I mean the city."

"We burnt it?"
        "Yes, you did."
                "But what a pity!
No wonder people hate us. But, I say,
I'll make your father like me yet, some day."

XXVIII

I settled down in Devon,
  When Johnnie went to France.
Such a tame ending
  To a great romance--
Two lonely women
  With nothing much to do
But get to know each other;
  She did and I did, too.
Mornings at the Rectory,
  Learning how to roll
Bandages, and always
  Saving light and coal.
Oh, that house was bitter
  As winter closed in,
In spite of heavy stockings
  And woolen next the skin.
I was cold and wretched,
  And never unaware
Of John more cold and wretched
  In a trench out there.

XXIX

All that long winter I wanted so much to complain,
But my mother-in-law, as far as I could see,
Felt no such impulse, though she was always in pain,
And, as the winter fogs grew thick,
Took to walking with a stick,
Heavily.
Those bubble-like eyes grew black
Whenever she rose from a chair--
Rose and fell back,
Unable to bear
The sure agonizing
Torture of rising.
Her hands, those competent bony hands,
Grew gnarled and old,
But never ceased to obey the commands
Of her will--only finding new hold
Of bandage and needle and pen.
And not for the blinking
Of an eye did she ever stop thinking
Of the suffering of Englishmen,
And her two sons in the trenches. Now and then
I could forget for an instant in a book or a letter,
But she never, never forgot--either one--
Percy and John--though I knew she loved one better--
Percy, the wastrel, the gambler, the eldest son.
I think I shall always remember
Until I die
Her face that day in December,
When in a hospital ward together, she and I
Were writing letters for wounded men and dying,
Writing and crying
Over their words, so silly and simple and loving,
Suddenly, looking up, I saw the old Vicar moving
Like fate down the hospital ward, until
He stood still
Beside her, where she sat at a bed.
"Dear friend, come home. I have tragic news," he said.

She looked straight at him without a spasm of fear,
Her face not stern or masked--
"Is it Percy or John?" she asked.
"Percy." She dropped her eyes. "I am needed here.
Surely you know
I cannot go
Until every letter is written. The dead
Must wait on the living," she said.
"This is my work. I must stay."
And she did--the whole long day.

XXX

Out of the dark, and dearth
Of happiness on earth,
Out of a world inured to death and pain;
On a fair spring morn
To me a son was born,
And hope was born--the future lived again.
To me a son was born,
The lonely hard forlorn
Travail was, as the Bible tells, forgot.
How old, how commonplace
To look upon the face
Of your first-born, and glory in your lot.

To look upon his face
And understand your place
Among the unknown dead in churchyards lying,
To see the reason why
You lived and why you die--
Even to find a certain grace in dying.

To know the reason why
Buds blow and blossoms die,
Why beauty fades, and genius is undone,
And how unjustified
Is any human pride
In all creation--save in this common one.

XXXI

Maternity is common, but not so
It seemed to me. Motherless, I did not know--
I was all unprepared to feel this glow,
Holy as a Madonna's, and as crude
As any animal's beatitude--
Crude as my own black cat's, who used to bring
Her newest litter to me every spring,
And say, with green eyes shining in the sun:
"Behold this miracle that I have done."

And John came home on leave, and all was joy
And thankfulness to me, because my boy
Was not a baby only, but the heir--
Heir to the Devon acres and a name
As old as England. Somehow I became
Almost an English woman, almost at one
With all they ever did--all they had done.

XXXII

"I want him called John after you, or if not that I'd rather. . . ."
"But the eldest son is always called Percy, dear."
"I don't ask to call him Hiram, after my father--"
"But the eldest son is always called Percy, dear."
"But I hate the name Percy. I like Richard or Ronald,
Or Peter like your brother, or Ian or Noel or Donald--"
"But the eldest is always called Percy, dear."

So the Vicar christened him Percy; and Lady Jean
Gave to the child and me the empty place
In hr heart. Poor Lady, it was as if she had seen
The world destroyed--the extinction of her race,
Her country, her class, her name--and now she saw
Them live again. And I would hear her say:
"No. I admire Americans; my daughter-in-law
Was an American." Thus she would well repay
The debt, and I was grateful--the English made
Life hard for those who did not come to her aid.

XXXIII

"They must come in in the spring."
  "Don't they care sixpence who's right?"
"What a ridiculous thing--
  Saying they're too proud to fight."

"Saying they're too proud to fight."
  "Wilson's pro-German, I'm told."
"No, it's financial."
          "Oh, quite,
  All that they care for is gold."

"All that they care for is gold."
  "Seem to like writing a note."
"Yes, as a penman, he's bold."
  "No. It's the Irish vote."

"Oh, it's the Irish vote."
  "What if the Germans some night
Sink an American boat?"
  "Darling, they're too proud to fight."

XXXIV

What could I do, but ache and long
That my country, peaceful, rich, and strong,
Should come and do battle for England's sake.
What could I do, but long and ache.
And my father's letters I hid away
Lest some one should know the things he'd say.
"You ask me whether we're coming in--
We are. The English are clever as sin,
Silently, subtly they inspire
Most of our youth with a holy fire
To shed their blood for the British Empire.
We'll come in--we'll fight and die
Humbly to help them, and by and by,
England will do us in the eye.
They'll get colonies, gold and fame,
And we'll get nothing at all but blame.
Blame for not having come before,
Blame for not having sent them more
Money and men and war supplies,
Blame if we venture to criticize.
We're so damn simple--our skins so thin
We'll get nothing whatever, but we'll come in."

XXXV

And at last--at last--like the dawn of a calm, fair day
After a night of terror and storm, they came--
My young light-hearted countrymen, tall and gay,
Looking the world over in search of fun and fame,
Marching through London to the beat of a boastful air,
Seeing for the first time Piccadilly and Leicester Square,
All the bands playing: "Over There, Over There,
Send the word, send the word to beware--"
And as the American flag went fluttering by
Englishmen uncovered, and I began to cry.

XXXVI

"We're here to end it, by jingo."
  "We'll lick the Heinies okay."
"I can't get on to the lingo."
  "Dumb--they don't get what we say."

"Call that stuff coffee? You oughter
  Know better. Gee, take it away."
"Oh, for a drink of ice water!"
  "They think nut-sundae's a day!"

"Say, is this chicken feed money?"
  "Say, does it rain every day?"
"Say, Lady, isn't it funny,
  Everyone drives the wrong way?"

XXXVII

How beautiful upon the mountains,
How beautiful upon the downs,
How beautiful in the village post office,
On the pavements of towns--
How beautiful in the huge print of newspapers,
Beautiful while telegraph wires hum,
While telephone bells wildly jingle,
The news that peace has come--
That peace has come at last--that all wars cease.
How beautiful upon the mountains are the footsteps
Of the messengers of peace!

XXXVIII

In the depth of the night betwixt midnight and morning,
  In the darkness and silence forerunning the dawn,
The throb of my heart was a drum beat of warning,
  My ears were a strain, and my breath was undrawn.

In the depth of the night, when the old house was sleeping,
  I lying alone in a desolate bed,
Heard soft on the staircase a slow footstep creeping--
  The ear of the living--the step of the dead.

In the depth of the night betwixt midnight and morning
  A step drawing near on the old oaken floor--
On the stair--in the gallery--the ghost that gives warning
  Of death, by that heartbreaking sigh at my door.

XXXIX

Bad news is not broken,
  By kind tactful word.
The message is spoken
  Ere the word can be heard.
The eye and the bearing,
  The breath make it clear,
And the heart is despairing
  Before the ears hear.
I do not remember
  The words that they said:
"Killed--Douai--November--"
  I knew John was dead.
All done and over--
  That day long ago--
The white cliffs of Dover--
  Little did I know.

XL

As I grow older, looking back, I see
Not those the longest planted in the heart
Are the most missed. Some unions seem to be
Too close for even death to tear apart.
Those who have lived together many years,
And deeply learnt to read each other's mind,
Vanities, tempers, virtues, hopes, and fears--
One can not go--nor is one left behind.
Alas, with John and me this was not so;
I was defrauded even of the past.
Our days had been so pitifully few,
Fight as I would, I found the dead go fast.
I had lost all--had lost not love alone,
But the bright knowledge it had been my own.

XLI

Oh, sad people, buy not your past too dearly,
  Live not in dreams of the past, for understand,
If you remember too much, too long, too clearly,
  If you grasp memory with too heavy a hand,
You will destroy memory in all its glory
  For the sake of the dreams of your head upon your bed.
You will be left with only the worn dead story
  You told yourself of the dead.

XLII

Nanny brought up my son, as his father before him,
  Austere on questions of habits, manners, and food.
Nobly yielding a mother's right to adore him,
  Thinking that mothers never did sons much good.

A Scot from Lady Jean's own native passes,
  With a head as smooth and round as a silver bowl,
A crooked nose, and eyes behind her glasses
  Gray and bright and wise--a great soul!
Ready to lay down her life for her charge, and ready
  To administer discipline without consulting me:
"Is that the way for you to answer my leddy?
  I think you'll get no sweet tonight to your tea."

Bringing him up better than I could do it,
  Teaching him to be civil and manly and cool
In the face of danger. And then before I knew it
  The time came for him to go off to school.

Off to school to be free of women's teaching,
  Into a world of men--at seven years old;
Into a world where a mother's hands vainly reaching
  Will never again caress and comfort and hold.

XLIII

My father came over now and then
To look at the boy, and talk to me,
Never staying long,
For the urge was strong
To get back to his yawl and the summer sea.
He came like a nomad passing by,
Hands in his pockets, hat over one eye,
Teasing every one great and small
With a blank straight face and a Yankee drawl;
Teasing the Vicar on Apostolic Succession
And what the Thirty-Nine Articles really meant to convey,
Teasing Nanny, though he did not
Make much impression
On that imperturbable Scot.
Teasing our local grandee, a noble peer,
Who firmly believed the Ten Lost Tribes
Of Israel had settled here--
A theory my father had at his fingers' ends--
Only one person was always safe from his jibes--
My mother-in-law, for they were really friends.

XLIV

Oh, to come home to your country
  After long years away,
To see the tall shining towers
  Rise over the rim of the bay,
To feel the west wind steadily blowing
  And the sunshine golden and hot,
To speak to each man as an equal,
  Whether he is or not.

XLV

Was this America--this my home
Prohibition and Teapot Dome--
Speakeasies, night clubs, illicit stills,
Dark faces peering behind dark grills,
Hold-ups, kidnappings, hootch or booze--
Everyone gambling--you just can't lose,
Was this my country? Even the bay
At home was altered, strange ships lay
At anchor, deserted day after day,
Old yachts in a rusty dim decay--
Like ladies going the primrose way--
At anchor, until when the moon was black,
They sailed, and often never came back.

Even my father's Puritan drawl
Told me shyly he'd sold his yawl
For a fabulous price to the constable's son--
My childhood's playmate, thought to be one
Of a criminal gang, rum-runners all,
Such clever fellows with so much money--
Even the constable thought it funny,
Until one morning his son was found,
Floating dead in Long Island Sound.
Was this my country? It seemed like heaven
To get back, dull and secure, to Devon,
Loyally hiding from Lady Jean
And my English friends the horrors I'd seen.

XLVI

That year she died, my nearest, dearest friend;
Lady Jean died, heroic to the end.
The family stood about her grave, but none
Mourned her as I did. After, one by one,
They slipped away--Peter and Bill--my son
Went back to school. I hardly was aware
Of Percy's lovely widow, sitting there
In the old room, in Lady Jean's own chair.

An English beauty glacially fair
Was Percy's widow Rosamund, her hair
Was silver gilt, and smooth as silk, and fine,
Her eyes, sea-green, slanted away from mine,
From anyone's, as if to meet the gaze
Of others was too intimate a phase
For one as cool and beautiful as she.

We were not friends or foes. She seemed to be
Always a little irked--fretted to find
That other women lived among mankind.
Now for the first time after years of meeting,
Never exchanging more than formal greeting,
She spoke to me--that sharp determined way
People will speak when they have things to say.

XLVII

ROSAMUND: Susan, go home with your offspring. Fly.
Live in America.
SUSAN: Rosamund, why?

ROSAMUND: Why, my dear girl, haven't you seen
What English country life can mean
With too small an income to keep the place
Going? Already I think I trace
A change in you, you no longer care
So much how you look or what you wear.
That coat and skirt you have on, you know
You wouldn't have worn them ten years ago.
Those thick warm stockings--they make me sad,
Your ankles were ankles to drive men mad.
Look at your hair--you need a wave.
Get out--go home--be hard--be brave,
Or else, believe me, you'll be a slave.
There's something in you--dutiful--meek--
You'll be saving your pin-money every week
To mend the roof. Well, let it leak.
Why should you care?

SUSAN: But I do care,
John loved this place, and my boy's the heir.

ROSAMUND: The heir to what? To a tiresome life
Drinking tea with the Vicar's wife,
Opening bazaars, and taking the chair
At meetings for causes that you don't care
Sixpence about and never will;
Breaking your heart over every bill.
I've been in the States, where everyone,
Even the poor, have a little fun.
Don't condemn your son to be
A penniless country squire. He
Would be happier driving a tram over there
Than moldering his life away as heir.

40

SUSAN: Rosamund dear, this may all be true.
I'm an American through and through.
I don't see things as the English do,
But it's clearly my duty, it seems to me,
To bring up John's son, like him, to be
A country squire--poor, alas,
But true to that English upper class
That does not change and does not pass.

ROSAMUND: Nonsense; it's come to an absolute stop,
Twenty years since we sat on top
Of the world, amusing ourselves and sneering
At other manners and customs, jeering
At other nations, living in clover--
Not any more. That's done and over.
No one nowadays cares a button
For the upper classes--they're dead as mutton.
Go home.

SUSAN: I notice that you don't go.

ROSAMUND: My dear, that shows how little you know.
I'm escaping the fate of my peers,
Marrying one of the profiteers,
Who hasn't an "aitch" where an "aitch" should be,
But millions and millions to spend on me.
Not much fun--but there wasn't any
Other way out. I haven't a penny.
But with you it's different. You can go away,
And oh, what a fool you'd be to stay.

XLVIII

Rabbits in the park,
  Scuttling as we pass,
Little white tails
  Against the green grass.
"Next time, Mother,
I must really bring my gun,
  I know you don't like shooting,
But . . ."
          John's own son.
That blond bowed face,
  Those clear steady eyes,
Hard to be certain
  That the dead don't rise.
Jogging on his pony
  Through the autumn day,
"Bad year for fruit, Mother,
  But good salt hay."
Bowling for the village
  As his father had before;
Coming home at evening
  To read the cricket score,
Back to the old house
  Where all his race belong,
Tired and contented--
  Rosamund was wrong.

XLIX

If some immortal strangers walked our land
And heard of death, how could they understand
That we--doomed creatures--draw our meted breath
Light-heartedly--all unconcerned with death.
So in these years between the wars did men
From happier continents look on us when
They brought us sympathy, and saw us stand
Like the proverbial ostrich--head in sand--
While youth passed resolutions not to fight,
And statesmen muttered everything was right--
Germany, a kindly, much ill-treated nation--
Russia was working out her own salvation
Within her borders. As for Spain, ah, Spain
Would buy from England when peace came again!
I listened and believed--believed through sheer
Terror. I could not look whither my fear
Pointed--that agony that I had known.
I closed my eyes, and was not alone.

Later than many, earlier than some,
I knew the die was cast--that war must come;
That war must come. Night after night I lay
Steeling a broken heart to face the day
When he, my son--would tread the very same
Path that his father trod. When the day came
I was not steeled--not ready. Foolish, wild
Words issued from my lips--"My child, my child,
Why should you die for England too?" He smiled:
"Is she not worth it, if I must?" he said.
John would have answered yes--but John was dead.

43

L

Is she worth dying for? My love, my one
And only love had died, and now his son
Asks me, his alien mother, to assay
The worth of England to mankind today--
This other Eden, demi-paradise,
This fortress built by Nature for herself
Against infection and the hand of war;
This happy breed of men, this little world,
This precious stone set in the silver sea--
Ah, no, not that--not Shakespeare--I must be
A sterner critic. I must weigh the ill
Against the good, must strike the balance, till
I know the answer--true for me alone--
What is she worth--this country--not my own?

I thought of my father's deep traditional wrath
Against England--the redcoat bully--the ancient foe--
That second reaping of hate, that aftermath
Of a ruler's folly and ignorance long ago--
Long, long ago--yet who can honestly say
England is utterly changed--not I--not I.
Arrogance, ignorance, folly are here today.
And for these my son must die?
I thought of these years, these last dark terrible years
When the leaders of England bade the English believe
Lies as the price of peace, lies and fears,
Lies that corrupt, and fears that sap and deceive.
I thought of the bars dividing man from man,
Invisible bars that the humble may not pass,
And how no pride is uglier, crueler than
The pride unchecked of class.
Oh, those invisible bars of manners and speech,
Ways that the proud man will not teach
The humble lest they too reach
Those splendid heights where a little band
Have always stood and will always stand
Ruling the fate of this small green land,

Rulers of England--for them must I
Send out my only son to die?

LI

And then, and then,
I thought of Elizabeth stepping down
Over the stones of Plymouth town
To welcome her sailors, common men,
She herself, as she used to say,
Being "mere English" as much as they--
Seafaring men who sailed away
From rocky inlet and wooded bay,
Free men, undisciplined, uncontrolled,
Some of them pirates and all of them bold,
Feeling their fate was England's fate,
Coming to save it a little late,
Much too late for the easy way,
Much too late, and yet never quite
Too late to win in that last worst fight.

And I thought of Hampden and men like him,
St John and Eliot, Cromwell and Pym,
Standing firm through the dreadful years,
When the chasm was opening, widening,
Between the Commons and the King;
I thought of the Commons in tears--in tears,
When Black Rod knocked at Parliament's door,
And they saw Rebellion straight before--
Weeping, and yet as hard as stone,
Knowing what the English have always known
Since then--and perhaps have known alone--
Something that none can teach or tell--
The moment when God's voice says; "Rebel."

Not to rise up in sudden gust
Of passion--not, though the cause be just;
Not to submit so long that hate,

Lava torrents break out and spill
Over the land in a fiery spate;
Not to submit forever, until
The will of the country is one man's will,
And every soul in the whole land shrinks
From thinking--except as his neighbor thinks.
Men who have governed England know
That dreadful line that they may not pass
And live. Elizabeth long ago
Honored and loved, and bold as brass,
Daring and subtle, arrogant, clever,
English, too, to her stiff backbone,
Somewhat a bully, like her own
Father--yet even Elizabeth never
Dared to oppose the sullen might
Of the English, standing upon a right.

LII

And were they not English, our forefathers, never more
English than when they shook the dust of her sod
From their feet forever, angrily seeking a shore
Where in his own way a man might worship his God.
Never more English than when they dared to be
Rebels against her--that stem intractable sense
Of that which no man can stomach and still be free,
Writing: "When in the course of human events . . ."
Writing it out so all the world could see
Whence come the powers of all just governments.
The tree of Liberty grew and changed and spread,
But the seed was English.

I am American bred,
I have seen much to hate here--much to forgive,
But in a world where England is finished and dead,
I do not wish to live.

THE END

46

Also from Benediction Books ...
Wandering Between Two Worlds: Essays on Faith and Art
Anita Mathias
Benediction Books, 2007
152 pages
ISBN: 0955373700

Available from www.amazon.com, www.amazon.co.uk

In these wide-ranging lyrical essays, Anita Mathias writes, in lush, lovely prose, of her naughty Catholic childhood in Jamshedpur, India; her large, eccentric family in Mangalore, a sea-coast town converted by the Portuguese in the sixteenth century; her rebellion and atheism as a teenager in her Himalayan boarding school, run by German missionary nuns, St. Mary's Convent, Nainital; and her abrupt religious conversion after which she entered Mother Teresa's convent in Calcutta as a novice. Later rich, elegant essays explore the dualities of her life as a writer, mother, and Christian in the United States-- Domesticity and Art, Writing and Prayer, and the experience of being "an alien and stranger" as an immigrant in America, sensing the need for roots.

About the Author

Anita Mathias is the author of *Wandering Between Two Worlds: Essays on Faith and Art.* She has a B.A. and M.A. in English from Somerville College, Oxford University, and an M.A. in Creative Writing from the Ohio State University, USA. Anita won a National Endowment of the Arts fellowship in Creative Nonfiction in 1997. She lives in Oxford, England with her husband, Roy, and her daughters, Zoe and Irene.

Visit Anita's website
    http://www.anitamathias.com,
and Anita's blog
    http://dreamingbeneaththespires.blogspot.com, (Dreaming Beneath the Spires).

The Church That Had Too Much
Anita Mathias
Benediction Books, 2010
52 pages
ISBN: 9781849026567

Available from www.amazon.com, www.amazon.co.uk

The Church That Had Too Much was very well-intentioned. She wanted to love God, she wanted to love people, but she was both hampered by her muchness and the abundance of her possessions, and beset by ambition, power struggles and snobbery. Read about the surprising way The Church That Had Too Much began to resolve her problems in this deceptively simple and enchanting fable.

About the Author

Anita Mathias is the author of *Wandering Between Two Worlds: Essays on Faith and Art.* She has a B.A. and M.A. in English from Somerville College, Oxford University, and an M.A. in Creative Writing from the Ohio State University, USA. Anita won a National Endowment of the Arts fellowship in Creative Nonfiction in 1997. She lives in Oxford, England with her husband, Roy, and her daughters, Zoe and Irene.

Visit Anita's website
    http://www.anitamathias.com,
and Anita's blog
    http://dreamingbeneaththespires.blogspot.com (Dreaming Beneath the Spires).

CPSIA information can be obtained at www.ICGtesting.com
Printed in the USA
LVOW07*1439161014

409090LV00006B/35/P